ODE TO WALT WHITMAN
•
FIRST SONGS
•
A FLOOD OF TEARS FOR IGNACIO SANCHEZ MEJIAS
•
SIX GALICIAN POEMS

ODE TO WALT WHITMAN
and Other Poems

Federico García Lorca

Translated by
Carlos Bauer

City Lights Books
San Francisco

Library of Congress Cataloging-in-Publication Data
García Lorca, Federico, 1898-1936.
   [Poems. English & Spanish. Selections]
   Ode to Walt Whitman & other poems/by Federico García Lorca; trans-
lated by Carlos Bauer.
          p.   cm.
ISBN 0-87286-212-7 (pbk.): $6.95
   1. García Lorca, Federico, 1898-1936 — Translations, English. I. Bauer,
Carlos. II. Title. III. Title: Ode to Walt Whitman and other poems.
PQ6613.A763A213 1988
861' .62 — dc19   88-2586 CIP

City Lights Books are available to bookstores through our primary distrib-
utor: Subterranean Company, P.O. Box 10233, Eugene OR 97440 [503]
343-6324. Our books are also available through library jobbers and regional
distributors. For personal orders and catalogs, please write to City Lights
Books, 261 Columbus Avenue, San Francisco, CA 94133.

CITY LIGHTS BOOKS are edited by Lawrence Ferlinghetti and Nancy J.
Peters and published at the City Lights Bookstore, 261 Columbus Avenue,
San Francisco, CA 94133.

CONTENTS

INTRODUCTION

The four books of poetry presented in this volume span the most creative period of Federico García Lorca's life, and transport us through the poet's major stylistic transitions from the "brief poem," which marked his earliest work, through a middle period, where his poetry became much more complex, and, finally, his return to Spanish folklore as an inspiration, and to a less intricate verse structure and simpler language.

Because of their relative briefness, these four books never achieved the wide circulation of some of his other books, yet they contain some of the finest poetry Lorca wrote.

FIRST SONGS

This book is both a work-in-progress and, in retrospect, an anthology. Of the sixteen poems included in *First Songs*, thirteen belong to a projected work entitled *Suites* which Lorca had intended to complete one day. In his last known interview, he told the Argentinian journalist Otero Seco that it was "a book I've worked on a great deal, and with much love, about ancient themes." How close to finishing the book is not known, as no final, or near-final, manuscript has ever been found. Of the other three poems in the volume, "Adam," "Captive," and "Song," two found their way into other works, though Lorca may have considered including them in *Suites*. "Adam" almost certainly would have formed part of another projected book, *Sonnets of Dark Love*, just as "Song" first formed part of the provisional contents of *Earth and Moon* and then finally became part of *Divan of the Tamarit* under a new title: *Casida of the Dark Doves*. "Captive," on the other hand, has not been found in any other manuscripts. Thus, *First Songs* is exactly what the publisher, Manuel Altolaguirre, stated in his brief introductory note: ". . . a book from his adolescence still not put in final order by its author . . ." and, ". . . a foretaste of a more extensive and representative collection." Ten years after *Poem of the Deep Song* was written, Lorca put it into definitive form, making no extensive changes in the poems themselves but rather arranging them into a coherent whole. That, probably, would also have been the case with the poems in *First Songs*.

The idea of publishing *First Songs* appears to have come about sometime in late 1932 or early 1933. In 1944, in reminiscences about García Lorcia, Manuel Altolaguirre related a part of that genesis: "It seems like yesterday he came to see me, just before my first child was born, the one that died. He brought me his first songs as a gift. 'For your child, I want to give him my first verses, which have never been published.' " The first child of Concha Méndez and Manuel Altolaguirre was born dead in March of 1933. Further on, Altolaguirre continues: "How much I liked having him give me those first poems of his for my first born! 'With whatever book sales produce, you buy your child what you most desire.' It seems like I'm viewing his papers now, all so tiny, creased, written in pencil. . . except for one poem, the sonnet "Adam," which I believe to be from a later date than the songs." In the first draft of the article, Altolaguirre went into more detail, stating that all the manuscript sheets were turning yellow with age, save the sonnet "Adam," which later was discovered to have been written in 1929, when the poet was in New York. The editor's note gives 1922 as the date of composition (the date Lorca himself probably gave Altolaguirre), although most of the poems were actually written in the summer of 1921.

First Songs, probably planned for 1933, came out some three years later. A few months after Lorca brought Altolaguirre the manuscript, the latter was given a grant by the Spanish government to study English publishing and did not return to Spain until the spring of 1935. Finally, on January 28, 1936, Ediciones Héroe, which Altolaguirre called his "small revolutionary publishing house," brought out *First Songs*. (Héroe, though small and short-lived, published works by some of the greatest poets of the 20th century: Pablo Neruda, Rafael Alberti, Luis Cernuda, Pedro Salinas, and Miguel Hernández.)

In 1921, a crucial year, García Lorca found his true voice as a poet. That year, he wrote his first masterpiece, *Poem of the Deep Song*, and began writing the first poems of *First Songs*. In the latter, he transports us to a softer world, to a timeless Andalusia of vivid landscapes, where only occasionally do we spy the underlying despair of frustrated love, and the terrifying reality that all of us, alone in the universe, face in the end.

ODE TO WALT WHITMAN

Almost in desperation, and consumed by pessimism (brought on by a failed love affair and a devastating identity crisis), Federico García Lorca set off for New York with his friend and mentor, the professor Fernando de los Ríos, in the early summer of 1929. New York, it now appears, was an escape for Lorca; he could just as well have gone anywhere. Once there, however, Lorca's Andalusian soul recoiled from that strident environment: the pitiless heart of American capitalism. In New York, he saw the future of the world: a terrifying mercantile nightmare; and man's fate: a complete divorcement from nature. Only a few months later would come the Crash of '29 and the Great Depression. Out of that chaos — and his own personal crises — was born what has come to be called Lorca's "New York Cycle" of poems. His *Ode to Walt Whitman* is one of the most important, if not the most important poem in that series, for Lorca fashions a near perfect synthesis of personal preoccupations (the homosexual question) and universal questions (the future of mankind under capitalism), using a meditation on the Camden poet as the vehicle.

Over the last fifteen years or so, the most well-known book to have come out of the New York Cycle, *Poet in New York*, has drawn fire over questions of its textual integrity and its organization: Was *Poet in New York*, published almost simultaneously in Mexico and the United States in 1940, merely a compilation — and a bad one, at that — made by Lorca's then-exiled Spanish publisher, José Bergamín? And why did the two published texts differ so greatly, when, after all, Bergamín was the one who supplied the text used for both editions? Did Bergamín do some heavy-handed and unjustified editing?[1] Were some of the poems included in *Poet in New York* really intended by Lorca for another book, *Earth and Moon*, which the poet had spoken about in his last known interview? Today, close to fifty years after its publication, one cannot help but conclude that any version of *Poet in*

New York is still only provisional.

While the posthumous *Poet in New York* and the theoretical *Earth and Moon* must be viewed as somewhat less than definitive, Lorca did in fact publish one book during his life that used material from his New York cycle: *Ode to Walt Whitman*. In Mexico, Ediciones Alcancía, under the direction of Justino Fernández and Edmundo O'Gorman, published a limited edition of some fifty copies in 1933. Lorca himself was well satisfied with the book, illustrated by Rodríguez Lozano, telling friends he thought it "exquisite." *Ode to Walt Whitman* thus appears to be, until new information is uncovered, the one work to have come out of his New York poems that can be judged both structurally and textually definitive.

The original manuscript bears the date of June 15 [1930], which places Lorca in Havana, where he spent several months after leaving the United States that spring, or possibly aboard ship in route back to Spain. The date shows that *Ode to Walt Whitman* was written at the time of his other great meditation on homosexual love, his drama *The Public*.[2] Lorca had been pondering the homosexual question for some time, and he had come to firm conclusions for his life and works. What a few critics claim to be his ambivalence about homosexual love in *Ode to Walt Whitman* is rather a firm call for — or a return to — an all-encompassing pansexualism. As one of Lorca's most perceptive interpreters, the writer Paco Umbral, has noted: "With his condemnation of the homosexuals of the city [...] Lorca is [in effect] composing a song to that other superior form of homosexuality, which has its illustrious precedent in Ancient Greece..." And a little further on Umbral concludes: "Lorca censures citified homosexuality because he believes homosexuality to be one [of many] natural acts on the broad canvas of nondogmatic nature. When homosexuality is locked up behind doors and concealed within the society that proscribes it, it then turns into something clandestine and sinful. It loses its grandeur, it becomes degraded."[3]

In final analysis, Lorca places the blame on capitalism for turning America (where even "Jews were selling the rose of circumcision") into a country that is "inundated with machines and tears"; and for turning Whitman's love, Whitman's dreams — the ones found in the "Calamus" poems — into just another debased currency.

A FLOOD OF TEARS FOR IGNACIO SANCHEZ MEJIAS

On August 11, 1934, at five in the afternoon, the traditional start of bullfights, in the plaza of Manzanares, the famous *torero* Ignacio Sánchez Mejías topped the bill. He had been called in to substitute for Domingo Ortega, who had been injured in an automobile accident. The day before, Sánchez Mejías had fought in faraway Huesca, but that is the lot of the bullfighter, who travels the circuit from town to town. Sánchez Mejías would face the first bull of the day, "Granadino."

The first *tercio*, the first third of the bullfight, went well for Sánchez Mejías. His passes demonstrated the bravery that marked his style. (Bullfight critics of the early twenties had written of his relentless search for danger in the ring, and how that had given something completely new to the spectacle.) Now the crowd was with him: Ignacio had always had to conquer the crowd as well as the bull he was fighting.

Then came the *picador* on his horse, driving the lance deep into the bull's back. Then the *banderillas* were placed.

The final *tercio* began. Sánchez Mejías would make his first passes *en estribo*: sitting on a narrow wooden plank that runs inside the wall of the ring about eighteen inches above the ground, and is used to jump out of the ring. His first pass went off perfectly. Then the bull charged him again, this time from left to right. He repeated his previous maneuver, but this time the bull's right horn caught him and tossed him into the air. Lying in the sand, Sánchez Mejías bled profusely while the others in his *cuadra* got the bull away from him.

Once in the infirmary, they cut open his pant leg and cleaned the blood off. The gore wound was five to six inches deep into his right thigh, up near the groin. The infirmary doctor had only to take one look to pronounce the wound serious. And, quickly, it was decided to speed the *torero* to the hospital in Madrid, 200 kilometers away.

Sánchez Mejías did not arrive there until one the next morning. He suffered through the next day, was given a transfusion, and that night gangrene set in. The following morning he was dead. His body would be taken to his native Sevilla, and entombed next to his brother-in-law, one of the greatest *toreros* of all time, Joselito.

In 1927, Ignacio Sánchez Mejías gave up bullfighting, and had only returned to the profession a few months before his death. He was overweight and had lost much of his former agility. Why, then, did he return? Some say because he needed the money; others, that he needed danger, the excitement of the bullring. Whatever the reason (and, more than likely, it was a combination of both), there can be no doubt that Sánchez Mejías had been an adventurer — and a man of action — his whole life. Even though born into a wealthy family (his father was a well-known physician), Ignacio always sought more than a bourgeois life could give him. Even as a child, he courted risk and romance; his playmates were the kids of the street who were to become flamenco singers, or bullfighters, or petty thieves.

At seventeen, he ran away from home to become a bullfighter in Mexico. There he started out as a *banderillo*, and not until the early twenties did he come into his own as a *torero*, after a decade learning his art at the side of the finest bullfighters of his time. While critics never considered him to be the best of his age, it should be noted that the two *toreros* who were better than him, Joselito and Belmonte, are conceded to be the greatest bullfighters of all time, and Sánchez Mejías did in fact earn a place alongside them on bullfight cards and in the hearts of bullfight *aficionados*.

Sánchez Mejías achieved fame as a *torero*, yet was not just another bullfighter. From the early twenties he counted poets and playwrights as friends, and became especially close to Lorca, Rafael Alberti, and other young poets of the Generation of 1927. (With Lorca he shared a love of traditional Andalusian music and folklore; and he even attempted to turn Alberti into a bullfighter.) And Sánchez Mejías turned to writing. In 1925, some two years before he left bullfighting for the first time, he gave a reading in Valladolid of two chapters from his never-to-be-finished novel, which many — and not only his friends — judged to be excellent. Then, in 1928, his drama *Sinrazón* — the first attempt ever at Freudian theater in Spanish letters — met with high praise in the Madrid press. Later that same year, his light comedy *Zaya* was produced, and it, too, was well received. 1929 found him in New York with his *compañera* "La Argentinita," the dancer Encarnación López Júlvez (who also was a close friend of Lorca's, and to whom this poem is dedicated), where he had been invited to lecture on bullfighting and the spectacle surrounding the *lidia*. There they saw Lorca often and, once back in Spain, their friendship deepened and in the years that followed, the three collaborated on important cultural projects.

Ignacio Sánchez Mejías had been a hero to a generation of poets because he was the prototype of that rare individual who could fuse into one complex personality the man of action and the contemplative man of letters. In the chaos-filled 1930s, it seems only fitting that Sánchez Mejías returned to a profession defined by violence and death. Yet, perhaps what is most important about the man can only be discerned in the stupefying absence his death left in the hearts of those who had known him and had become his friends.

A Flood of Tears for Ignacio Sánchez Mejías was published as a book in 1935, less than a year after the death of the *torero*, by the prestigious house Cruz y Raya, under the direction of Lorca's close friend José Bergamín.[4] Most critics consider it Lorca's finest poem. It combines traditional elements found in early works, like *Poem of the Deep Song* and *Gypsy Romances*, with the superrealism of his New York cycle of poems. Even in the key word of the title, *Llanto* (a copious amount of tears, accompanied by sobs and wailing), Lorca unites ancient and modern. We know from his brother Francisco that he wanted to avoid using the word *elegía* (elegy); in his choice of the modern term *llanto* Lorca conjures from the past the echo of the *plantos*, elegies, or laments, of the middle ages. How Lorca carries the medieval *planto* into a modern context is illustrated in this comparison — one many Lorca scholars have noted — between a fragment of Jorge Manrique's *Coplas* and Lorca's lines in the "*Llanto por Ignacio Sánchez Mejías.*"

Manrique:

A friend to friends,
what a Lord for Servants
and kinsmen!
what an enemy of our enemies!
what a teacher for the valiant
and the courageous!

Lorca:

What a great fighter in the ring!
What a mountaineer in the mountains!
How very soft with the wheat!
How very hard with his spurs!
How tender with the dew drops!
How dazzling on fair days!
How tremendous with those final
banderillas of twilight!

On hearing of Sánchez Mejías' decision to return to the bullring, Lorca is reputed to have said: "Ignacio has just announced his death to me ...!" When he heard of Ignacio's death, Rafael Alberti wrote to a friend: "What horror!"

Ignacio Sánchez Mejías was dead at forty-three, leaving behind a glorious career in the bullring, marked by tremendous bravery and heart. The literary man left a series of articles on bullfighting, two fine plays, an unfinished novel — and a deep sorrow in the hearts of two of Spain's greatest poets, which, in turn, led to two of the finest elegies ever written. Alberti wrote *Verte y no verte* (*To See You and Not See You*):

> (*Upon the Black Sea, a ship*
> *is traveling to Rumania.*
> *Over waterless routes*
> *travels your mortal agony.*
> *To see you and not see you.*
> *Me, navigating far, far away;*
> *and you, through death.*)

And Lorca wrote what one critic, Rafael Martínez Nadal, called the most desolate elegy in all of Spanish literature:

> Neither bull nor the fig tree knows you,
> neither horses nor the ants of your home.
> Neither child nor the afternoon knows you,
> because you have died for all time.

SIX GALICIAN POEMS

Galicia, in the extreme northwestern part of Spain, is a region of deep, dark and luxuriant green landscapes; rains sweep in perpetually from grey, winter-time seas. A land of thick fogs rolling in from the Bay of Biscay, of afternoon mists or hazy sunlight. In the center of Galicia lies Santiago de Compostela, after Jerusalem and Rome the most important Christian place of pilgrimage of the Middle Ages. Supposedly, in the ninth century, the tomb of the apostle St. James the Greater was miraculously discovered, and the king of Asturias, Alfonso II, built a shrine around which the city of Santiago grew up. The people of Galicia are of Celtic stock, for the most part, and the language they speak evolved from Galician-Portuguese, which extended over all of Galicia and most of Portugal in ancient times. On the Iberian peninsula, Galicia is as far away as one can get geographically, if not spiritually, from Lorca's Granada.

The first Galician literature is found in the few surviving remnants of the troubadours, when the Galician-Portuguese language predominated in vast areas of the peninsula. Then, as the Spanish state began to form under the dominance of Castillian kings, Galician gave way to Castillian, which became the official language of the realm. By the fifteenth century, Galicia had been so isolated, both politically and culturally, that the Galician language had almost disappeared as a written language, and was relegated to colloquial use, to the home.

Then, in the early 1800s, Galician had a resurgence. With the French invasion of the peninsula, Galicia was more or less abandoned to its own fate, and out of that came Galician nationalism and a flowering of culture and language. Short periods of freedom and self-rule were followed by harsh periods of intellectual repression. This heightened Galician self-awareness, which gave birth to a literature of protest, whose basic themes were the poverty and neglect that the region suffered, and the never-ending need for Galician men to emigrate to provide bare subsistence for their families.

One name stood out above all others in the period of Galician literary revival, that of Rosalía de Castro (1837-1885). Both a novelist and poet, writing in Galician and Castillian, Rosalía de Castro sought her roots in Galician customs and language. In 1860, she went with her husband to live in Madrid. Her feeling of isolation there, and her nostalgia for her homeland, mark the poems of *Cantares Galegos*, a major work in her native language. Her poetry cries out against the poverty and injustice inflicted on the Galician people, and their forced cultural assimilation. As a youth, Lorca had read Rosalía de Castro and her influence can be seen throughout his work. The alienation experienced by Galicia's seafarers and emigrants in the poetry of Rosalía de Castro is much the same as that of Lorca's Gypsies, Harlem blacks, and homosexuals. *Six Galician Poems* is, in a very real sense, an homage to Rosalía de Castro.

From 1931, García Lorca made a number of trips to Galicia with the university theater group he directed, "La Barraca," which took classical Spanish theater to the far corners of Spain. The overpowering landscape and the spoken Galician tongue — the most inherently poetic language on the Iberian peninsula — must have profoundly affected Lorca. One of his Galician friends of those years relates: "[Lorca] told us that in some localities of the Sierra of Granada he had known people and communities of Galician origin — descendants of the repopulators after the Reconquest — who still conserved words, expressions and songs of their forefathers." Thus, it is not strange that Lorca would feel compelled to create a mythical Galicia in much the same way he created his mythical Andalusia.

Lorca began writing the first poems of this volume in 1931, and probably finished *Six Galician Poems* sometime in 1934. One poem, *Cántiga of the Young Shopboy*, was almost definitely written after he had traveled to Buenos Aires in late 1933, where he came into contact with the large Galician immigrant community. Then, at the end of July, 1935, Lorca gave the poet, journalist and director of the publishing house "Nos," Eduardo Blanco-Amor, the manuscript of *Six Galician Poems*. It consisted, according to Blanco-Amor, of an odd assortment of sheets — one poem written on an invitation to lunch with the Portuguese ambassador; another written across the typed side of a royalty statement from the Spanish Society of Playwrights; one on an envelope, a card still inside; and so on. At the end of December, 1935, Nos published the short volume, with an introduction by Blanco-Amor.

Six Galician Poems never achieved the prominence it deserved. Within a few months, the Spanish Civil War broke out, leaving little time for this short book to be appreciated. During the war, Galicia remained under Francoist control, and afterwards, Lorca became a non-person in Spain, and books in Galician were prohibited by the Franco government. In recent years, *Six Galician Poems* has finally begun to be viewed as a major achievement in Galician letters. Today most anthologies of Galician poetry include a selection of Lorca's poems.

With six poems Lorca transports us across the Galician landscape, both geographic and spiritual, and even into the sad, lonesome world of Galician emigration...and then we can even hear the words of Rosalía de Castro upon the bitter, rain-filled winds: "Poor Galicia, never must you call yourself Spanish...your people scattered throughout the world, while you, sad and alone, only implore God for hope..."

Carlos Bauer

1. In all fairness to Bergamín (the conscience of Spanish intellectuals during the forty-year struggle against Spanish fascism), not one scholar brought up any of these questions until some thirty years after the fact, by which time Bergamín was well over seventy, and the rest of his collaborators were all dead.

2. Federico García Lorca, *The Public and Play without a Title: Two Posthumous Plays* (New York: New Directions, 1983).

3. Francisco Umbral, *Lorca, poeta maldito* (Barcelona: Bruguera, 1978), p.p. 137-8.

4. This book was the finest edition of Lorca's work published during his lifetime. The first printing consisted of some 2,000 copies, then a vast amount for a book of poetry. It came out as part of Cruz y Raya's most important imprint: Ediciones del Arbol. The book was also illustrated by three drawings done by the then eighteen-year-old painter José Caballero, who had collaborated with Lorca in the traveling student theater group *La Barraca*.

PRIMERAS CANCIONES
FIRST SONGS

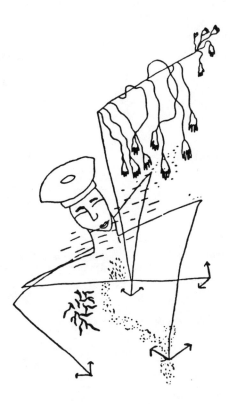

REMANSOS

[Ciprés]

Ciprés.
(Agua estancada.)

Chopo.
(Agua cristalina.)

Mimbre.
(Agua profunda.)

Corazón.
(Agua de pupila.)

STILL POOLS

[*Cypress*]

Cypress.
(Stagnant water.)

Poplar.
(Crystalline water.)

Willow.
(Deep water.)

Heart.
(Water of the pupil.)

REMANSILLO

Me miré en tus ojos
pensando en tu alma.

Adelfa blanca.

Me miré en tus ojos
pensando en tu boca.

Adelfa roja.

Me miré en tus ojos.
¡Pero estabas muerta!

Adelfa negra.

TINY STILL POOL

I saw myself in your eyes,
thinking about your soul.

White oleander.

I saw myself in your eyes,
thinking about your mouth.

Red oleander.

I saw myself in your eyes.
But you were already dead!

Black oleander.

VARIACION

El remanso del aire
bajo la rama del eco.

El remanso del agua
bajo fronda de luceros.

El remanso de tu boca
bajo espesura de besos.

VARIATION

That still pool of the air
under the branch of an echo.

That still pool of the water
under a frond of bright stars.

That still pool of your mouth
under a thicket of kisses.

REMANSO, CANCION FINAL

Ya viene la noche.

Golpean rayos de luna
sobre el yunque de la tarde.

Ya viene la noche.

Un árbol grande se abriga
con palabras de cantares.

Ya viene la noche.

Si tú vinieras a verme
por los senderos del aire.

Ya viene la noche.

Me encontrarías llorando
bajo los álamos grandes.
¡Ay morena!
Bajo los álamos grandes.

STILL POOL, A FINAL SONG

Here comes the night.

The moonbeams beat down
upon the anvil of evening.

Here comes the night.

A huge tree wraps itself
in the words of canticles.

Here comes the night.

If you came to visit me
on the paths of the winds.

Here comes the night.

You would find me weeping
under the big black poplars.
Oh, dark-haired girl!
Under the big black poplars.

MEDIA LUNA

La luna va por el agua.
¿Cómo está el cielo tranquilo?
Va segando lentamente
el temblor viejo del río
mientras que una rana joven
la toma por espejito.

HALF MOON

The moon goes over the water.
How can the sky be so tranquil?
She sets about slowly reaping
the river's ancient tremor
while a young frog takes her
for a tiny little mirror.

CUATRO BALADAS AMARILLAS

A Claudio Guillén

I

En lo alto de aquel monte
hay un arbolito verde.

Pastor que vas,
pastor que vienes.

Olivares soñolientos
bajan al llano caliente.

Pastor que vas,
pastor que vienes.

Ni ovejas blancas ni perro,
ni cayado, ni amor tienes.

Pastor que vas.

Como una sombra de oro
en el trigal te disuelves.

Pastor que vienes.

FOUR YELLOW BALLADS

To Claudio Guillén

I

On top of that mountain
there is a tiny green tree.

> *Shepherd who comes,*
> *shepherd who goes.*

Dreamy olive groves
descend to the hot plain.

> *Shepherd who comes,*
> *shepherd who goes.*

Neither white sheep nor a dog,
neither staff nor love, have you.

> *Shepherd who comes.*

Like a golden shadow in some
wheat field, you dissolve.

> *Shepherd who goes.*

II

La tierra estaba
amarilla.

Orillo, orillo,
pastorcillo.

Ni luna blanca
ni estrella lucían.

Orillo, orillo,
pastorcillo.

Vendimiadora morena
corta el llanto de la viña.

Orillo, orillo,
pastorcillo.

II

The earth was
yellow.

>   A *fringe, a fringe,*
>   *a shepherd all a-twinge.*

Neither white moon
nor star was shimmering.

>   A *fringe, a fringe,*
>   *a shepherd all a-twinge.*

Dark girl of the vineyard,
cut the tears from the vine.

>   A *fringe, a fringe,*
>   *a shepherd all a-twinge.*

III

Dos bueyes rojos
en el campo de oro.

Los bueyes tienen ritmo
de campanas antiguas
y ojos de pájaro.
Son para las mañanas
de niebla, y sin embargo,
horadan la naranja
del aire, en el verano.
Viejos desde que nacen
no tienen amo.
Y recuerdan las alas
de sus costados.
Los bueyes
siempre van suspirando
por los campos de Ruth
en busca del vado,
del eterno vado,
borrachos de luceros
a rumiarse sus lllantos.

Dos bueyes rojos
en el campo de oro.

III

Two reddish oxen
in fields of gold.

The oxen have a rhythm
of ancient church bells,
and eyes of a bird.
Suited for mist-laden
mornings, and nonetheless,
they pierce the oranges
of the wind in summer.
Old since their birth,
they have no master.
And they recall the wings
of their ancestors.
The oxen
go about forever sighing
through the fields of Ruth
in search of the ford,
that eternal ford,
drunk on bright stars,
to ruminate on their tears.

Two reddish oxen
in fields of gold.

IV

Sobre el cielo
de las margaritas ando.

Yo imagino esta tarde
que soy santo.
Me pusieron la luna
en las manos.
Yo la puse otra vez
en los espacios,
y el Señor me premió
con la rosa y el halo.

Sobre el cielo
de las margaritas ando.

Y ahora voy
por este campo.
A librar a las niñas
de galanes malos
y dar monedas de oro
a todos los muchachos.

Sobre el cielo
de las margaritas ando.

IV

Upon a sky
of daisies go I.

This evening I imagine
that I am a saint.
They placed the moon
into my hands.
I put it back again,
out in space;
and the Lord rewarded me
with a rose and a halo.

Upon a sky
of daisies go I.

And now I travel
through these fields:
To free young girls
from evil suitors,
and to give gold coins
to all the young boys.

Upon a sky
of daisies go I.

PALIMPSESTOS

A José Moreno Villa

I

Ciudad

El bosque centenario
penetra en la ciudad
pero el bosque está dentro
del mar.

Hay flechas en el aire
y guerreros que van
perdidos entre ramas
de coral.

Sobre las casas nuevas
se mueve un encinar
y tiene el cielo enormes
curvas de cristal.

PALIMPSESTS

To José Moreno Villa

I

City

The century-old forest
penetrates into the city,
yet the forest is inside of
the sea.

There are arrows in the air,
and warriors who go about
lost among the branches
of coral.

Above the new houses
sways a grove of oaks;
and the sky has enormous
curves of crystal.

II

Corredor

Por los altos corredores
se pasean dos señores

> (*Cielo*
> *nuevo.*
> *¡Cielo*
> *azul!*)

. . .se pasean dos señores
que antes fueron blancos monjes

> (*Cielo*
> *medio.*
> *¡Cielo*
> *morado!*)

. . .se pasean dos señores
que antes fueron cazadores

> (*Cielo*
> *viejo.*
> *¡Cielo*
> *de oro!*)

. . .se pasean dos señores
que antes fueron. . .

> (*Noche.*)

II

Mountain Pass

Through the high passes
two gentlemen are strolling

(*New*
sky.
Blue
sky!)

...two gentlemen are strolling
who before were white monks

(*Half*
sky.
Purple
sky!)

...two gentlemen are strolling
who before were hunters

(*Old*
sky.
Gold
sky!)

...two gentlemen are strolling
who before were...

(*Night.*)

III

Primera página

A Isabel Clara
mi ahijada

Fuente clara.
Cielo claro.

¡Oh, cómo se agrandan
los pájaros!

Cielo claro.
Fuente clara.

¡Oh, cómo relumbran
las naranjas!

Fuente.
Cielo.

¡Oh, cómo el trigo
es tierno!

Cielo.
Fuente.

¡Oh, cómo el trigo
es verde!

III

First Page

To Isabel Clara
my goddaughter

Clear spring.
Clear sky.

Oh, how the birds grow
so large!

Clear sky.
Clear spring.

Oh, how the oranges shine
so bright!

Spring.
Sky.

Oh, how the wheat
is so tender!

Sky.
Spring.

Oh, how the wheat
is so green!

ADAN

Arbol de sangre moja la mañana
por donde gime la recién parida.
Su voz deja cristales en la herida
y un gráfico de hueso en la ventana.

Mientras la luz que viene fija y gana
blancas metas de fábula que olvida
el tumulto de venas en la huida
hacia el turbio frescor de la manzana,

Adán sueña en la fiebre de la arcilla
un niño que se acerca galopando
por el doble latir de su mejilla.

Pero otro Adán oscuro está soñando
nuetra luna de piedra sin semilla
donde el niño de luz se irá quemando.

ADAM

A tree of blood dampened the morning's glow;
nearby a new-born woman cried and swooned.
Her voice left glass deep inside the wound,
and a pale outline of bones upon the window.

While the light steadily comes and overtakes
the pure aims of a fable that always forsakes
the turmoil of veins in its hurried flight
to the apple's turbid chill and its delight,

Adam dreams, in his fever of clay so alone,
of a tiny child who now approaches galloping
over the throbbing flesh of his cheekbone.

But another one, a dark Adam, sits dreaming
of a moon without seed, neutered and of stone,
where a child of light is forever left burning.

CLARO DE RELOJ

Me senté
en un claro del tiempo.
En un remanso
de silencio,
de un blanco silencio,
anillo formidable
donde los luceros
chocaban con los doce flotantes
números negros.

PAUSE OF THE CLOCK

I sat down
inside a pause in time.
In a still pool
of silence:
a formidable ring,
where bright stars
crashed into the twelve black,
floating numerals.

CAUTIVA

Por las ramas
indecisas
iba una doncella
que era la vida.
Por las ramas
indecisas.
Con un espejito
reflejaba el día
que era un resplandor
de su frente limpia.
Por las ramas
indecisas.
Sobre las tinieblas
andaba perdida,
llorando rocío,
del tiempo cautiva.
Por las ramas.
indecisas.

CAPTIVE

Among the hesitant
branches
went a maiden
who was life.
Among the hesitant
branches.
With a tiny mirror
she reflected the day,
which was the sparkle
of her clear brow.
Among the hesitant
branches.
Upon the dark of night
she walked about lost,
weeping dewdrops
of this captive time.
Among the hesitant
branches.

CANCION

Por las ramas del laurel
vi dos palomas oscuras.
La una era el sol,
la otra la luna.
Vecinitas, les dije,
¿dónde está mi sepultura?
En mi cola, dijo el sol.
En mi garganta, dijo la luna.
Y yo que estaba caminando
con la tierra a la cintura
vi dos águilas de mármol
y una muchacha desnuda.
La una era la otra
y la muchacha era ninguna.
Aguilitas, les dije,
¿dónde está mi sepultura?
En mi cola, dijo el sol.
En mi garganta, dijo la luna.
Por las ramas del cerezo
vi dos palomas desnudas.
La una era la otra
y las dos eran ninguna.

SONG

In the laurel branches,
I spied two dark doves.
The one was the sun;
the other, the moon.
Little neighbor ladies, I said:
O where lies my tomb?
In my tail, said the sun.
In my throat, said the moon.
And I, who was walking
with the earth to my waist,
spied two eagles of marble
and a naked young girl.
The one was the other,
and the girl was neither.
Little eagles, I said to them:
O where lies my tomb?
In my tail, said the sun.
In my throat, said the moon.
In the cherry tree branches,
I spied two naked doves.
The one was the other,
and both were neither one.

ODA A WALT WHITMAN
ODE TO WALT WHITMAN

1934

ODA A WALT WHITMAN

Por el East River y el Bronx
los muchachos cantaban enseñando sus cinturas.
Con la rueda, el aceite, el cuero y el martillo
noventa mil mineros sacaban la plata de las rocas
y los niños dibujaban escaleras y perspectivas.

Pero ninguno se dormía,
ninguno quería ser río,
ninguno amaba las hojas grandes,
ninguno la lengua azul de la playa.

Por el East River y el Queensborough
los muchachos luchaban con la industria,
y los judíos vendían al fauno del río
la rosa de la circuncisión,
y el cielo desembocaba por los puentes y los tejados
manadas de bisontes empujadas por el viento.

Pero ninguno se detenía,
ninguno quería ser nube,
ninguno buscaba los helechos
ni la rueda amarilla del tamboril.

Cuando la luna salga,
las poleas rodarán para turbar el cielo;
un límite de agujas cercará la memoria
y los ataúdes se llevarán a los que no trabajan.

ODE TO WALT WHITMAN

Along the East River and in the Bronx
young men were singing, showing off their waists.
With the wheel, the oil, the leather and the hammer,
ninety thousand miners extracted the silver from rocks,
and little boys were drawing stairs and perspectives.

But not one would sleep,
not one wished to be a river,
not one loved the great leaves,
not one, the blue tongue of the beach.

Along the East River and on the Queensborough
young men wrestled with industry,
and Jews were selling the rose of circumcision
to the faun of the river,
and the sky emptied out onto bridges and roofs
herds of bison pushed along by the winds.

But not one would ever pause,
not one wished to be a cloud,
not one searched for the fern
or the yellow wheel of the tambour.

When the moon comes out,
the pulleys will turn to disturb the skies;
a boundary of needles will enclose the memory,
and coffins will carry away those who never work.

Nueva York de cieno,
Nueva York de alambre y de muerte:
¿Qué ángel llevas oculto en la mejilla?
¿Qué voz perfecta dirá las verdades del trigo?
¿Quién, el sueño terrible de tus anémonas manchadas?

Ni un solo momento, viejo hermoso Walt Whitman,
he dejado de ver tu barba llena de mariposas,
ni tus hombros de pana gastados por la luna,
ni tus muslos de Apolo virginal,
ni tu voz como una columna de ceniza;
anciano hermoso como la niebla,
que gemías igual que un pájaro
con el sexo atravesado por una aguja.
Enemigo del sátiro.
Enemigo de la vid,
y amante de los cuerpos bajo la burda tela.

Ni un solo momento, hermosura viril,
que en montes de carbón, anuncios y ferrocarriles,
soñabas ser un río y dormir como un río
con aquel camarada que pondría en tu pecho
un pequeño dolor de ignorante leopardo.

Ni un solo momento, Adán de sangre, Macho,
hombre solo en el mar, viejo hermoso Walt Whitman,
porque por las azoteas,
agrupados en los bares,
saliendo en racimos de las alcantarillas,
temblando entre las piernas de los chauffeurs
o girando en las plataformas del ajenjo,
los maricas, Walt Whitman, te señalan.

New York of muck,
New York of wire and of death:
What angel is carried hidden in your cheek?
What perfect voice will speak the truths of the wheat?
Who, that terrible dream of your stained windflowers?

Not for one single moment, beautiful old Walt Whitman,
have I ever ceased seeing your beard full of butterflies,
or your corduroy shoulders worn thin by the moonlight,
or your thighs of a virginal Apollo,
or your voice just like a column of ash;
aged one, as beautiful as the mists,
who wailed the same as a bird
with its sex pierced by a needle.
Enemy of the satyr.
Enemy of the vine,
and lover of bodies beneath coarse cloth.

Not for one single moment, my virile beauty,
for on mountains of coal, on signs and on railroads,
you dreamed of being a river and sleeping like a river
next to that comrade who placed in your breast
the tiny hurts of nescient leopards.

Not for one single moment, Adam-blooded one, All-Male,
man alone upon the seas, beautiful old Walt Whitman,
because on rooftop terraces,
huddled together in bars,
running out of the sewers in bunches,
trembling between the legs of chauffeurs
or flitting about on the platforms of absinthe,
the faggots, Walt Whitman, are pointing at you.

¡También ése! ¡También! Y se despeñan
sobre tu barba luminosa y casta
rubios del Norte, negros de la arena,
muchedumbre de gritos y ademanes,
como los gatos y como las serpientes,
los maricas, Walt Whitman, los maricas,
turbios de lágrimas, carne para fusta,
bota o mordisco de los domadores.

¡También ése! ¡También! Dedos teñidos
apuntan a la orilla de tu sueño
cuando el amigo come tu manzana
con un leve sabor de gasolina,
y el sol canta por los ombligos
de los muchachos que juegan bajo los puentes.

Pero tú no buscabas los ojos arañados
ni el pantano oscurísimo donde sumergen a los niños,
ni la saliva helada,
ni las curvas heridas como panza de sapo
que llevan los maricas en coches y en terrazas
mientras la luna los azota por las esquinas del terror.

Tú buscabas un desnudo que fuera como un río.
Toro y sueño que junte la rueda con el alga,
padre de tu agonía, camelia de tu muerte,
y gimiera en las llamas de tu Ecuador oculto.

Porque es justo que el hombre no busque su deleite
en la selva de sangre de la mañana próxima.
El cielo tiene playas donde evitar la vida
y hay cuerpos que no deben repetirse en la Aurora.

That one, too! Him, too! And hurling themselves
down upon your luminous and chaste beard
are blonds of the north, Negroes of the sands;
a multitude of shrieks and gestures,
just like cats and just like snakes,
are the faggots, Walt Whitman, the faggots,
blurry-eyed with tears, flesh for the whip,
or the boot or the bite of animal trainers.

That one, too! Him, too! Tinted fingers
are leveled at the shores of your dream
when that friend eats from your apple
with its slight taste of gasoline,
and sunlight sings upon the navels
of the boys playing beneath the bridges.

But you never sought out scratched eyes
or the darkest swamps where they submerge little boys,
or that frozen saliva,
or those wounded curves like toads' bellies
that faggots lug about in cars and on terraces
while the moonlight lashes them on the street
    corners of terror.

You only sought a nude who would be like a river.
A bull and a dream that would join wheel and seaweed,
a sire of your mortal agony, a camillia of your death,
and he would wail in the flames of your hidden Equator.

Because it's not right for a man to seek his delight
in those blood jungles of the morning after.
The skies have shores where one can avoid life,
and some bodies should never be repeated in the Dawn.

Agonía, agonía, sueño, fermento y sueño.
Este es el mundo, amigo: agonía, agonía.
Los muertos se descomponen bajo el reloj de las ciudades.
La guerra pasa llorando con un millón de ratas grises,
los ricos dan a sus queridas
pequeños moribundos iluminados,
y la Vida no es noble, ni buena, ni sagrada.

Puede el hombre, si quiere, conducir su deseo
por vena de coral o celeste desnudo;
mañana los amores serán rocas y el Tiempo
una brisa que viene dormida por las ramas.

Por eso no levanto mi voz, viejo Walt Whitman,
contra el niño que escribe
nombre de niña en su almohada,
ni contra el muchacho que se viste de novia
en la oscuridad del ropero,
ni contra los solitarios de los casinos
que beben con asco el agua de la prostitución,
ni contra los hombres de mirada verde
que aman al hombre y queman sus labios en silencio.
Pero sí contra vosotros, maricas de las ciudades
de carne tumefacta y pensamiento inmundo.
Madres de lodo. Arpías. Enemigos sin sueño
del Amor que reparte coronas de alegría.

Agony, mortal agony, dream, ferment and dream.
That's the world, friend: agony, mortal agony.
The dead are decomposing beneath the clocks of the cities.
The war passes by us, weeping, with a million grey rats,
rich men give to their mistresses
tiny, illuminated half-corpses,
and Life is neither noble, nor good, nor sacred.

A man can, if he wishes, guide his desire
over a vein of coral or a celestial nude;
tomorrow loves will become rocks, and Time,
a breeze coming through the branches fast asleep.

That's why I never raise my voice, old Walt Whitman,
against the little boy who inscribes
a little girl's name deep into his pillow,
nor against the young man who dresses up as a bride
in the darkness of his clothes closet,
nor against those lonesome men of the casinos,
who drink with disgust from the waters of prostitution,
nor against those men with lecherous gazes,
who love men, but whose lips burn in silence.
But decidedly against you, faggots of the cities,
with your tumescent flesh and vile thoughts.
Mothers of filth. Harpies. Unsleeping enemies
of the Love that bestows crowns of joy.

Contra vosotros siempre, que dais a los muchachos
gotas de sucia muerte con amargo veneno.
Contra vosotros siempre,
"Fairies" de Norteamérica,
"Pájaros" de La Habana,
"Jotos" de Méjico,
"Sarasas" de Cádiz,
"Apios" de Sevilla,
"Cancos" de Madrid,
"Floras" de Alicante,
"Adelaidas" de Portugal.

¡Maricas de todo el mundo, asesinos de palomas!
Esclavos de la mujer. Perras de sus tocadores.
Abiertos en las plazas, con fiebre de abanico
o emboscados en yertos paisajes de cicuta.

¡No haya cuartel! La muerte
mana de vuestros ojos
y agrupa flores grises en la orilla del cieno.
¡No haya cuartel! ¡¡Alerta!!
Que los confundidos, los puros,
los clásicos, los señalados, los suplicantes
os cierren las puertas de la bacanal.

Forever against you, who give to all those young men,
drop by drop, the bitter venom of a foul death.
Forever against you,
Fairies of North America,
Pájaros of Havana,
Jotos of Mexico,
Sarasas of Cádiz,
Apios of Sevilla,
Cancos of Madrid,
Floras of Alicante,
Adelaidas of Portugal.

Faggots of the whole world, murderers of doves!
Slaves of women. Bitches of their boudoirs.
Openly in plazas, with a fever of fans,
or lying in ambush in the rigid landscapes of hemlock.

No quarter'll be given! Death
oozes from your eyes
and arranges grey flowers on the shores of the muck.
No quarter'll be given! Watch out!!
May the confused ones, the pure ones,
the classical ones, distinguished ones, imploring ones,
slam the gates of the bacchanal in your faces.

Y tú, bello Walt Whitman, duerme orillas del Hudson
con la barba hacia el Polo y las manos abiertas.
Arcilla blanda o nieve, tu lengua está llamando
camaradas que velen tu gacela sin cuerpo.

Duerme: no queda nada.
Una danza de muros agita las praderas
y América se anega de máquinas y llanto.
Quiero que el aire fuerte de la noche más honda
quite flores y letras del arco donde duermes,
y un niño negro anuncie a los blancos del oro
la llegada del reino de la espiga.

And you, beautiful Walt Whitman, sleep now next
    to the Hudson,
with your beard towards the Pole and your hands open wide.
In soft clay or in the snow, your tongue calls out to
those comrades keeping vigil over your bodiless gazelle.

Sleep now: nothing at all is left.
A dance of walls now shakes the meadows,
and America is inundated with machines and tears.
I wish the strong winds of that deepest of nights
would rip flower and letter from the arch where you sleep,
and that a black boy might announce to the whites of gold
the coming reign of the wheat.

LLANTO POR
IGNACIO SANCHEZ MEJIAS

A FLOOD OF TEARS
FOR IGNACIO SANCHEZ MEJIAS

A mi querida amiga
Encarnación López Júlvez

LLANTO
POR IGNACIO SANCHEZ MEJIAS

1

LA COGIDA Y LA MUERTE

A las cinco de la tarde.
Eran las cinco en punto de la tarde.
Un niño trajo la blanca sábana
a las cinco de la tarde.
Una espuerta de cal ya prevenida
a las cinco de la tarde.
Lo demás era muerte y sólo muerte
a las cinco de la tarde.

El viento se llevó los algodones
a las cinco de la tarde.
Y el óxido sembró cristal y níquel
a las cinco de la tarde.
Ya luchan la paloma y el leopardo
a las cinco de la tarde.
Y un muslo con un asta desolada
a las cinco de la tarde.
Comenzaron los sones de bordón
a las cinco de la tarde.
Las campanas de arsénico y el humo
a las cinco de la tarde.

A FLOOD OF TEARS
FOR IGNACIO SANCHEZ MEJIAS

1

HIS GORING AND HIS DEATH

At five in the afternoon.
It was five sharp in the afternoon.
A young boy brought the white sheet,
at five in the afternoon.
A basket of already waiting lime,
at five in the afternoon.
The rest was death and only death,
at five in the afternoon.

The wind carried off the cotton wool,
at five in the afternoon.
And the rust sowed glass and nickel,
at five in the afternoon.
Already dove and leopard are battling,
at five in the afternoon,
and a thigh with a desolate horn,
at five in the afternoon.
The sounds of bass strings commenced,
at five in the afternoon.
The bells of arsenic and the smoke,
at five in the afternoon.

En las esquinas grupos de silencio
a las cinco de la tarde.
¡Y el toro solo corazón arriba!
a las cinco de la tarde.
Cuando el sudor de nieve fue llegando
a las cinco de la tarde,
cuando la plaza se cubrió de yodo
a las cinco de la tarde,
la muerte puso huevos en la herida
a las cinco de la tarde.
A *las cinco de la tarde.*
A *las cinco en punto de la tarde.*

Un ataúd con ruedas es la cama
a las cinco de la tarde.
Huesos y flautas suenan en su oído
a las cinco de la tarde.
El toro ya mugía por su frente
a las cinco de la tarde.
El cuarto se irisaba de agonía
a las cinco de la tarde.
A lo lejos ya viene la gangrena
a las cinco de la tarde.
Trompa de lirio por las verdes ingles
a las cinco de la tarde.
Las heridas quemaban como soles
a las cinco de la tarde,
y el gentío rompía las ventanas
a las cinco de la tarde.
A las cinco de la tarde.
¡Ay, qué terribles cinco de la tarde!
¡Eran las cinco en todos los relojes!
¡Eran las cinco en sombra de la tarde!

On the corners, groups of silence,
at five in the afternoon.
And the bull alone with a high heart!
at five in the afternoon.
When the snowy sweat began arriving,
at five in the afternoon;
when the bullring was covered in iodine,
at five in the afternoon;
death laid its tiny eggs in the wound,
at five in the afternoon.
At *five in the afternoon.*
At *five sharp in the afternoon.*

A coffin on wheels is now his bed,
at five in the afternoon.
Bones and flutes sound in his ears,
at five in the afternoon.
The bull now bellows near his brow,
at five in the afternoon.
The room was iridescent with death throes,
at five in the afternoon.
From afar, the gangrene now approaches,
at five in the afternoon.
A trumpet of lilies in his green groin,
at five in the afternoon.
The wounds were burning him like suns,
at five in the afternoon,
and the throng was breaking the windows,
at five in the afternoon.
At five in the afternoon.
Oh, what a terrible five in the afternoon!
It was five on every one of the clocks!
It was five in the shade of the afternoon!

2

LA SANGRE DERRAMADA

¡Que no quiero verla!

Dile a la luna que venga,
que no quiero ver la sangre
de Ignacio sobre la arena.

¡Que no quiero verla!

La luna de par en par.
Caballo de nubes quietas,
y la plaza gris del sueño
con sauces en las barreras.

¡Que no quiero verla!
Que mi recuerdo se quema.
¡Avisad a los jazmines
con su blancura pequeña!

¡Que no quiero verla!

2

HIS SPILT BLOOD

No, I never want to see it!

Tell the moon to come quick,
for I never want to see Ignacio's
blood there upon the sand.

No, I never want to see it!

The moon, round and full.
A horse of stilled clouds,
and the grey bullring of dreams
with willows lining the barrier.

No, I never want to see it!
May my memory be consumed by fire.
Go and warn every jasmine,
in all their minute whiteness!

That I never want to see it!

La vaca del viejo mundo
pasaba su triste lengua
sobre un hocico de sangres
derramadas en la arena,
y los toros de Guisando,
casi muerte y casi piedra,
mugieron como dos siglos
hartos de pisar la tierra.
No.
¡Que no quiero verla!

Por las gradas sube Ignacio
con toda su muerte a cuestas.
Buscaba el amanecer,
y el amanecer no era.
Busca su perfil seguro,
y el sueño lo desorienta.
Buscaba su hermoso cuerpo
y encontró su sangre abierta.
¡No me digáis que la vea!
No quiero sentir el chorro
cada vez con menos fuerza;
ese chorro que ilumina
los tendidos y se vuelca
sobre la pana y el cuero
de muchedumbre sedienta.
¿Quién me grita que me asome?
¡No me digáis que la vea!

That cow of the ancient world
was running its sad tongue over
a snout covered in all the blood
spilt there upon the sand,
and those bulls of Guisando,
almost death and almost stone,
bellowed as if fed up with treading
the earth for two long centuries.
No.
No, I never want to see it!

Up through the tiers Ignacio climbs
with his whole death upon his back.
He was searching for daybreak,
yet daybreak it was not.
He seeks his staunch profile,
and his dream disorients him.
He sought his beautiful body
and found his blood in the open.
Never tell me to look at it!
I never want to feel the torrent,
all the time with less force;
that torrent which illuminates
the lower rows and spills onto
the corduroy and the leather
of a forever-thirsting crowd.
Who shouts for me to take a peek?
Never tell me to look at it!

No se cerraron sus ojos
cuando vio los cuernos cerca,
pero las madres terribles
levantaron la cabeza.
Y a través de las ganaderías
hubo un aire de voces secretas
que gritaban a toros celestes
mayorales de pálida niebla.

No hubo príncipe en Sevilla
que comparársele pueda,
ni espada como su espada
ni corazón tan de veras.
Como un río de leones
su maravillosa fuerza,
y como un torso de mármol
su dibujada prudencia.
Aire de Roma andaluza
le doraba la cabeza
donde su risa era un nardo
de sal y de inteligencia.
¡Qué gran torero en la plaza!
¡Qué buen serrano en la sierra!
¡Qué blando con las espigas!
¡Qué duro con las espuelas!
¡Qué tierno con el rocío!
¡Qué deslumbrante en la feria!
¡Qué tremendo con las últimas
banderillas de tiniebla!

His eyes never once closed
when he saw the horns so near,
but yet some terrible mothers
raised high their heads.
And all across the ranch lands
rose a draft of secret cries
shouted at celestial bulls
by foremen of pallid mist.

Never a prince in Sevilla
who could compare to him,
nor a sword like his sword,
nor a heart quite so true.
Just like a river of lions,
his marvelous strength;
and like a torso of marble,
his fine-drawn moderation.
An air of Andalusian Rome
would guild his head;
there his laughter became a nard
of both wit and intelligence.
What a great fighter in the ring!
What a mountaineer in the mountains!
How very soft with the wheat!
How very hard with his spurs!
How tender with the dew drops!
How dazzling on fair days!
How tremendous with those final
banderillas of twilight!

Pero ya duerme sin fin.
Ya los musgos y la hierba
abren con dedos seguros
la flor de su calavera.
Y su sangre ya viene cantando:
cantando por marismas y praderas,
resbalando por cuernos ateridos,
vacilando sin alma por la niebla,
tropezando con miles de pezuñas
como una larga, oscura, triste lengua,
para formar un charco de agonía
junto al Guadalquivir de las estrellas.
¡Oh blanco muro de España!
¡Oh negro toro de pena!
¡Oh sangre dura de Ignacio!
¡Oh ruiseñor de sus venas!
No.
¡Que no quiero verla!
Que no hay cáliz que la contenga,
que no hay golondrinas que la beban,
no hay escarcha de luz que la enfríe,
no hay canto ni diluvio de azucenas,
no hay cristal que la cubra de plata.
No.
¡¡Yo no quiero verla!!

But now he sleeps without end.
Already the moss and the grass,
with sure fingers, open up
the flower of his skull.
And now his blood comes singing:
singing over marshes and meadows,
gliding over horns frozen stiff,
wavering without a soul in the mist,
stumbling under thousands of hooves,
as if it were a long, dark, sad tongue,
and it forms a puddle of death throes
next to the Guadalquivir of the stars.
Oh, white wall of Spain!
Oh, black bull of sorrow!
Oh, hardened blood of Ignacio!
Oh, nightingale of his veins!
No.
No, I never want to see it!
Never a chalice big enough to contain it,
never any swallows that will drink it,
never a daylight frost to freeze it,
never a song or a deluge of lilies,
never crystal to plate it in silver.
No.
I never ever want to see it!!

3

CUERPO PRESENTE

La piedra es una frente donde los sueños gimen
sin tener agua curva ni cipreses helados.
La piedra es una espalda para llevar al tiempo
con árboles de lágrimas y cintas y planetas.

Yo he visto lluvias grises correr hacia las olas
levantando sus tiernos brazos acribillados,
para no ser cazadas por la piedra tendida
que desata sus miembros sin empapar la sangre.

Porque la piedra coge simientes y nublados,
esqueletos de alondras y lobos de penumbra;
pero no da sonidos, ni cristales, ni fuego,
sino plazas y plazas y otras plazas sin muros.

Ya está sobre la piedra Ignacio el buen nacido.
Ya se acabó. ¿Qué pasa? Contemplad su figura:
la muerte le ha cubierto de pálidos azufres
y le ha puesto cabeza de oscuro minotauro.

Ya se acabó. La lluvia penetra por su boca.
El aire como loco deja su pecho hundido,
y el Amor, empapado con lágrimas de nieve,
se calienta en la cumbre de las ganaderías.

A BODY LAID OUT

That stone is now a forehead where dreams lie moaning,
possessing neither curving water nor frozen cypress.
That stone is now a backbone on which time is borne,
with trees of tears and ribbons and planets.

I have seen grey rains running down to the waves
that raise their tender arms riddled with holes,
so never to be captured upon the laid-flat stone
that frees their limbs without soaking up the blood.

For the stone seizes onto seeds and cloud clusters,
the skeletons of larks and wolves of the twilight,
yet never produces sound, nor crystals, nor fire,
only bullrings and more rings and rings without walls.

Now upon that stone lies Ignacio the well-born.
It's over now. What's happening? Note his aspect:
death has covered him in pale sulphurs
and given him the head of a dark minotaur.

It's over now. Rain penetrates into his mouth.
The air rushes crazily from his sunken chest,
and Love, soaked through with tears of snow,
warms itself upon the summits of the ranch lands.

¿Qué dicen? Un silencio con hedores reposa.
Estamos con un cuerpo presente que se esfuma,
con una forma clara que tuvo ruiseñores
y la vemos llenarse de agujeros sin fondo.

¿Quién arruga el sudario? ¡No es verdad lo que dice!
Aquí no canta nadie, ni llora en el rincón,
ni pica las espuelas, ni espanta la serpiente:
aquí no quiero más que los ojos redondos
para ver ese cuerpo sin posible descanso.

Yo quiero ver aquí los hombres de voz dura.
Los que doman caballos y dominan los ríos:
los hombres que les suena el esqueleto y cantan
con una boca llena de sol y pedernales.

Aquí quiero yo verlos. Delante de la piedra.
Delante de este cuerpo con las riendas quebradas.
Yo quiero que me enseñen dónde está la salida
para este capitán atado por la muerte.

Yo quiero que me enseñen un llanto como un río
que tenga dulces nieblas y profundas orillas,
para llevar el cuerpo de Ignacio y que se pierda
sin escuchar el doble resuello de los toros.

Que se pierda en la plaza redonda de la luna
que finge cuando niña doliente res inmóvil;
que se pierda en la noche sin canto de los peces
y en la maleza blanca del humo congelado.

No quiero que le tapen la cara con pañuelos
para que se acostumbre con la muerte que lleva.
Vete, Ignacio: No sientas el caliente bramido.
Duerme, vuela, reposa: ¡También se muere el mar!

What're they saying? A stench-filled silence reposes.
We're here with a laid-out body starting to vanish,
with a clear shape that once possessed nightingales
and now we see it filling with bottomless holes.

Who dares crease the shroud? What he says isn't true!
Here nobody sings, or weeps off in some corner,
or pricks his spurs, or drives away the serpent:
here I wish for nothing more than my round eyes,
so I can view that body without any hope of rest.

I want to see, here, those men with harsh voices.
The ones who break horses and master the rivers:
those men whose skeletons resound, and who sing
with mouths full of sunlight and flints.

Here, I want to see them. In front of this stone.
Right in front of this body with its broken reins.
I want them to show me where there is a way out
for this captain bound tight by death.

I want them to show me a flood of tears like a river,
one that has gentle mists and steep banks,
to carry Ignacio's body away and then disappear
without ever hearing that double snort of the bulls.

May it disappear in the round bullring of the moon
that, as a child, pretends to be a hurt, still beast;
may it disappear into the songless night of the fish
and into that white thicket of the frozen smoke.

I never want them to cover his face with scarves,
so that he grows accustomed to the death he bears.
Go, now, Ignacio: Never listen to their hot bellow.
Sleep, take flight, repose: For the sea, too, shall die!

ALMA AUSENTE

No te conoce el toro ni la higuera,
ni caballos ni hormigas de tu casa.
No te conoce el niño ni la tarde
porque te has muerto para siempre.

No te conoce el lomo de la piedra,
ni el raso negro donde te destrozas.
No te conoce tu recuerdo mudo
porque te has muerto para siempre.

El Otoño vendrá con caracolas,
uva de niebla y montes agrupados,
pero nadie querrá mirar tus ojos
porque te has muerto para siempre.

Porque te has muerto para siempre,
como todos los muertos de la Tierra,
como todos los muertos que se olvidan
en un montón de perros apagados.

No te conoce nadie. No. Pero yo te canto.
Yo canto para luego tu perfil y tu gracia.
La madurez insigne de tu conocimiento.
Tu apetencia de muerte y el gusto de su boca.
La tristeza que tuvo tu valiente alegría.

Tardará mucho tiempo en nacer, si es que nace,
un andaluz tan claro, tan rico de aventura.
Yo canto su elegancia con palabras que gimen
y recuerdo una brisa triste por los olivos.

AN ABSENT SOUL

Neither bull nor the fig tree knows you,
neither horses nor the ants of your home.
Neither child nor the afternoon knows you,
because you have died for all time.

Neither the back of the stone knows you,
nor the black satin in which you crumble.
Nor even your mute remembrance knows you,
because you have died for all time.

The Autumn will arrive with its conches,
grapes of the mists and mountain clusters,
yet none will want to look you in the eye,
because you have died for all time.

Because you have died for all time,
the same as all the dead of this Earth,
the same as all the dead left forgotten
on a huge pile of lifeless dogs.

Nobody knows you. No. But I will sing of you.
Sing of your profile and grace for a later time.
Of that renowned maturity of your knowledge.
Your appetite for death and the taste of its mouth.
Of the sadness your joyous bravery once possessed.

A long time will pass before being born, if ever,
an Andalusian so open, so very rich in adventure.
I will sing of his elegance with words that wail,
and recall a sad breeze through the olive trees.

SEIS POEMAS GALEGOS
SIX GALICIAN POEMS

Federico García Lorca . 1935

MADRIGAL A CIBDA DE SANTIAGO

Chove en Santiago
meu doce amor.
Camelia branca do ar
brila entebrecido o sol.

Chove en Santiago
na noite escura.
Herbas de prata e sono
cobren a valdeira lúa.

Olla a choiva pola rúa,
laio de pedra e cristal.
Olla no vento esvaído
soma e cinza do teu mar.

Soma e cinza do teu mar
Santiago, lonxe do sol.
Ágoa de mañán anterga
trema no meu corazón.

MADRIGAL TO THE CITY
OF SANTIAGO

It's raining in Santiago,
sweet love of mine.
White camellia of the air,
obscurely shines the sun.

It's raining in Santiago
on this dark, dark night.
Grasses of silver and dream
cover the deserted moon.

See the rain on the streets:
an outcry of glass and stone.
See, in the vanishing winds,
the shadow and ash of your sea.

The shadow and ash of your sea,
Santiago, so far from the sun.
Water of an ancient morning
trembles deep within my heart.

ROMAXE DE NOSA SENORA DA BARCA

¡Ai *ruada, ruada, ruada*
da Virxen pequena
e a súa barca!

A Virxen era pequena
e a súa coroa de prata.
Marelos os catro bois
que no seu carro a levaban.

Pombas de vidro traguían
a choiva pola montana.
Mortas e mortos de néboa
polas congostras chegaban.

¡Virxen, deixa a túa cariña
nos doces ollos das vacas
e leva sobr'o teu manto
as frores da amortallada!

Pola testa de Galicia
xa ven salaiando a ialba.
A Virxen mira pra o mar
dend'a porta da súa casa.

¡Ai *ruada, ruada, ruada*
da Virxen pequena
e a súa barca!

ROMANCE FOR OUR LADY OF THE BOATS

Oh, revel, revel, revel,
for the tiny Virgin
and her boat!

The Virgin was so tiny,
and her silver crown, too.
Flaxen, those four oxen
pulling her in their cart.

Doves of crystal brought
rain through the mountains.
Dead men and women of mist
came down the narrow streets.

Virgin, leave your visage
upon the eyes of the cows,
and wear upon your mantle
the flowers of the shroud!

Over the brow of Galicia,
dawn now arrives sobbing.
The Virgin looks out to sea
from the doorway of her house.

Oh, revel, revel, revel,
for the tiny Virgin
and her boat!

CANTIGA DO NENO DA TENDA

A *Ernesto Pérez Guerra*

Bos Aires ten unha gaita
sobro do Río da Prata,
que a toca o vento do norde
coa súa gris boca mollada.
¡Triste Ramón de Sismundi!
Aló, na rúa Esmeralda,
basoira que te basoira
polvo d'estantes e caixas.
Ao longo das rúas infindas
os galegos paseiaban
soñando un val imposíbel
na verde riba da pampa.
¡Triste Ramón de Sismundi!
Sintéu a muiñeira d'ágoa
mentres sete bois de lúa
pacían na súa lembranza.
Foise pra veira do río,
veira do Río da Prata.
Sauces e cabalos múos
creban o vidro das ágoas.
Non atopóu o xemido
malencónico da gaita,
non víu o imenso gaiteiro
coa boca frolida d'alas;
triste Ramón de Sismundi,
veira do Río da Prata,
víu na tarde amortecida
bermello muro de lama.

74

CANTIGA OF THE YOUNG SHOPBOY

To Ernesto Pérez Guerra

Buenos Aires has a bagpipe
up above the River Plate,
which the north wind blows
with its damp, grey mouth.
Sad, sad Ramón de Sismundi!
There on Esmeralda Street
he cleans and cleans again
the dust from shelf and box.
Up and down infinite streets
the Galicians would stroll,
dreaming of impossible valleys
at the green edges of the Pampa.
Sad, sad Ramón de Sismundi!
He heard the water's *muiñeira*
while seven oxen of the moon
grazed in his remembrance.
He went down to the river,
down to the River Plate.
Willow trees and mute horses
break the water's fine crystal.
Never once he encountered
the bagpipe's melancholy whine,
never saw the immense piper
whose mouth flowered with wings;
sad, sad Ramón de Sismundi,
down by the River Plate, saw
in the dying light of evening
a bright red wall of mud.

NOITURNIO DO ADOESCENTE MORTO

Imos silandeiros orela do vado
pra ver o adoescente afogado.

Imos silandeiros veiriña do ar,
antes que ise río o leve pro mar.

Súa ialma choraba, ferida e pequena
embaixo os arumes de pinos e d'herbas.

Ágoa despenada baixaba da lúa
cobrindo de lirios a montana núa.

O vento deixaba camelias de soma
na lumieira murcha de súa triste boca.

¡Vinde mozos loiros do monte e do prado
pra ver o adoescente afogado!

¡Vinde xente escura do cume e do val
antes que ise río o leve pro mar!

O leve pro mar de curtiñas brancas
onde van e vén vellos bois de ágoa.

¡Ai, cómo cantaban os albres do Sil
sobre a verde lúa, coma un tamboril!

¡Mozos, imos, vinde, aixiña, chegar
porque xa ise río m'o leva pra o mar!

NOCTURNE OF
THE DEAD ADOLESCENT

Down to the ford, let's go silently.
and the drowned adolescent we'll see.

To the air's edge, let's go silently,
before the river takes him to the sea.

His soul was weeping, wounded and so tiny
beneath the aroma of pine trees and of grass.

Crashing waters descended from the moon,
covering the naked mountain with lilies.

The wind left camellias of shadow
in the withered light of his sad mouth.

Come, blond youths of mountain and meadow,
come and see the drowned adolescent!

Come, dark people of summits and valleys,
before this river takes him to the sea!

It carries him to a sea of white pastures,
where water oxen forever come and go.

Oh, how the Sil's trees sang in splendor
on that green moon, just like a tambour!

Boys, let's go, hurry up, fast, quickly,
for now this river carries me to the sea!

CANZON DE CUNA PRA ROSALIA CASTRO, MORTA

¡Érguete miña amiga
que xa cantan os galos do día!
¡Érguete miña amada
porque o vento muxe, coma unha vaca!

Os arados van e vén
dende Santiago a Belén.
Dende Belén a Santiago
un anxo ven en un barco.
Un barco de prata fina
que trai a door de Galicia.
Galicia deitada e queda
transida de tristes herbas.
Herbas que cobren teu leito
e a negra fonte dos teus cabelos.
Cabelos que van ao mar
onde as nubens teñen seu nidio pombal.

¡Érguete miña amiga
que xa cantan os galos do día!
¡Érguete miña amada
porque o vento muxe, coma unha vaca!

CRADLESONG FOR
A DEAD ROSALIA CASTRO

Arise, my dear friend,
for dawn's roosters now sing!
Arise, my dear beloved,
for the wind moos, just like a cow!

The ploughs come and go,
from Santiago to Bethlehem.
From Bethlehem to Santiago,
an angel is coming in a ship.
A ship made of fine silver,
that brings Galicia's sorrow.
Galicia laid-out and left
overwhelmed by sad grasses.
Grasses that cover your bed,
and the black source of your tresses.
Tresses that reach to the sea,
where the clouds have made their dovecote.

Arise, my dear friend,
for dawn's roosters now sing!
Arise, my dear beloved,
for the wind moos, just like a cow!

DANZA DA LUA
EN SANTIAGO

¡Fita aquel branco galán,
olla seu transido corpo!

É a lúa que baila
na Quintana dos mortos.

Fita seu corpo transido,
negro de somas e lobos.

Nai: A lúa está bailando
na Quintana dos mortos.

¿Quén fire potro de pedra
na mesma porta do sono?

¡É a lúa! ¡É a lúa
na Quintana dos mortos!

¿Quén fita meus grises vidros
cheos de nubens seus ollos?

É a lúa, é a lúa
na Quintana dos mortos.

Déixame morrer no leito
soñando con froles d'ouro.

Nai: A lúa está bailando
na Quintana dos mortos.

DANCE OF THE MOON IN SANTIAGO

Look at that white suitor,
observe his stricken body!

It's the moon dancing
in the Square of the Dead.

Look at his stricken body,
black with shadow and wolves.

Mother: The moon's dancing
in the Square of the Dead.

Who wounds a colt of stone
at the very gates of sleep?

It's the moon! It's the moon,
in the Square of the Dead!

Who looks in my grey windows,
his eyes filled with clouds?

It's the moon, it's the moon,
in the Square of the Dead.

Let me die there in my bed,
dreaming of golden flowers.

Mother: The moon is dancing
in the Square of the Dead.

¡Ai filla, co ar do ceo
vólvome branca de pronto!

Non é o ar, é a triste lúa
na Quintana dos mortos.

¿Quén brúa co-este xemido
d'imenso boi melancónico?

Nai: É a lúa, é a lúa
na Quintana dos mortos.

¡Sí, a lúa, a lúa
coronada de toxos,
que baila, e baila, e baila
na Quintana dos mortos!

Oh, child, with heaven's winds,
I'm turning white so quickly!

Not the wind, it's the sad moon
in the Square of the Dead.

Who's howling with that wail
of a huge melancholy ox?

Mother: It's the moon, the moon,
in the Square of the Dead.

Yes, it's the moon, the moon,
crowned with furze,
that dances, and dances, and dances,
in the Square of the Dead!

NOTES ON THE POEMS

Page 2. *Remansos* are the still pools in a larger body of water, such as the calm areas that form in a rushing river.

Page 57. The bulls of Guisando are prehistoric stone sculptures of four bulls, made by members of an ancient cult of the bull. They stand in a meadow near the village of Guisando in the province of Avila.

Page 57. Lorca uses the word "illuminate" in the sense of illuminating a manuscript.

Page 59. *Banderillas* are long decorated darts that are planted in the bull's shoulders and back during the bullfight.

Page 61. The Guadalquivir is the river that runs through Sevilla, Sánchez Mejías' native city.

Page 67. Conches are horns blown by shepherds in the countryside.

Page 67. The final line refers to Pino Montano, Sánchez Mejías' estate, which always held fond remembrances for Lorca.

Page 75. *Cántigas* are medieval Galician-Portuguese ballads.

Page 75. The *muiñeira* is a traditional Galician dance, with its accompanying music.

Page 77. The Sil River runs through the south of Galicia, meeting up with the Miño River, which then flows to the sea and forms part of the Spanish-Portuguese border.

Page 80. *Quintana dos mortos* refers to the plaza of the Quintana, in Santiago de Compostela, constructed over an ancient cemetery.